My Children's Horrific Journey to Freedom

ANDY LIEU

Thank you to Mr. Vito M, Tinaburri my personal editor for helping me better convey my story through heartfelt phrases while delivering the same message.

◆ FriesenPress

Suite 300 - 990 Fort St
Victoria, BC, V8V 3K2
Canada

www.friesenpress.com

Copyright © 2020 by Andy lieu
First Edition — 2020

All rights reserved.

No part of this publication may be reproduced in any form, or by any means, electronic or mechanical, including photocopying, recording, or any information browsing, storage, or retrieval system, without permission in writing from FriesenPress.

ISBN
978-1-5255-5165-9 (Hardcover)
978-1-5255-5166-6 (Paperback)
978-1-5255-5167-3 (eBook)

1. BIOGRAPHY & AUTOBIOGRAPHY, PERSONAL MEMOIRS

Distributed to the trade by The Ingram Book Company

CHAPTER 1

After the Americans left Vietnam

My Mother's Perspective

This is a true story of my two adolescent children's daring escape in 1978 from the North Vietnamese communist regime, following the Vietnam War. My son, Andy Lieu, was thirteen and my daughter, Allison Lieu, was seventeen at the time of their escape. The reason I'm sharing this is to impress upon other children and people living in free and democratic countries to cherish, to be grateful, and to be thankful for the gift of freedom that they enjoy every day.

I would wish that no human being would ever have to go through the nightmares that my children had to endure. The horror and multiple near-death experiences they suffered on their journey still haunt them today, still lingering in emotional scars.

Their journey encompassed the full spectrum of emotions: shock, sadness, horror, disappointment, fear, uncertainty, loss, desperation, hunger, hopelessness, anxiety, hardship, as well as excitement, joy, and happiness.

America's involvement in Vietnam, fighting against the uprising of Communism in Southeast Asia during the period 1955 to 1975, is well-known. One year after the Americans left Vietnam, the country fell into ruin and deteriorated into its worst shape ever. I was desperate to send my children out of the hopelessness dark future in communist Vietnam, where no opportunities for a good education existed, only brain washing in communist ideologies by the North Vietnamese communist regime.

My plan was to send my younger son, Warren, and my oldest daughter, Allison, across the border into China, and from China, migrate to Hong Kong and reach freedom. This would be the safest route as it would avoid both the dangers of the ocean and the merciless Thai pirates. This route would also avoid the Malaysian coast guards who were preventing escaping Vietnamese refugees from landing on the Malaysian coast. It would be much better for them to take the "China route" out of Vietnam as they were fluent in Chinese.

Unfortunately, the "China route" was a big mistake.

In Vietnam, people thought China would not be as bad as the living hell of Vietnam. They were wrong, they were badly wrong ... In China, my children experienced far worst living conditions than anyone could have ever imagined. They could not communicate back to me in Vietnam; the Vietnamese and Chinese Authorities would not allow any communication across the border because they were about to start a war. Eventually, war broke out in 1979.

At that time, China was like North Korea today: full of suffering, mental torture, and hopelessness. My children took the journey on their own, without knowing the danger.

My son Andy said to me, "Mom, God pulled me out of death three times on this journey. God saved me from hell again, again and again!" Andy will continue to tell the story of their horrific journey from here.

CHAPTER 2

After the Vietnam War Ended

This is how we started our "Journey to Freedom." We were living in a war-torn country. The Vietcong (the army and police force of the communist regime) were confiscating South Vietnamese citizens' possessions at gun point stealing their homes, their land, their money, their vehicles, their businesses, and their personal belongings. They stopped businesses from operating; they forced people out of their homes and into hard labour in the countryside without pay and with little food. It was difficult to survive.

Facing starvation and fearing for their lives, the South Vietnamese people were desperate and willing to risk everything to flee the country by boat, car, or any other means of escape.

Freedom is priceless yet it cost far more than anyone could have imagined. Many South Vietnamese gave up their families, their homes, and their country as they risked their lives escaping Vietnam. Many died at sea from drowning or starvation. Some Vietnamese boat people were even forced to eat the dead bodies of fellow countrymen in order to stay alive. ("Vietnamese boat people" is the name given to the Vietnamese refugees who fled Vietnam after the Vietnam war ended.)

Thai sea pirates robbed countless boats. Mercilessly, they raped, killed, or kidnapped the Vietnamese women; men and small children were drowned. The brutality of the pirates towards the helpless and dying Vietnamese refugees dissuaded people from escaping to Malaysia and Thailand. Some Vietnamese boat people escaped these murders and lived to tell their horrific stories. No country has ever brought the sea pirates to justice.

CHAPTER 3

The Escape Plans

In 1977, my mother's clothing business was confiscated at gun point. The North Vietnamese communist regime demanded that everyone be equal: no one was allowed to be richer than anyone else, thus, no businesses were permitted to operate. My mother was a single mom (my parents divorced due to my father's gambling problem) without an income and with six children to raise ...

My mom is very strong and resilient. Alone, she raised all six of her children and was able to bring home food and provide all of us with education. She even managed to save enough money for us to escape Vietnam so that we could have a better life and a better future in a free country.

My mother's plan was for us to escape Vietnam in two separate groups; if all seven of us escaped as one group and were caught by the Vietcong then we would be doomed forever, with no chance of rescue by a family member.

The Vietcong frequently set up escape plans in order to trap civilians wanting to leave the country by boat. The Vietcong would gather them into the boat, collect all the fees, and then signal the local coast guard to arrest the escapees when the boat was on the way to the ocean. During the arrest, the Vietcong would confiscate all the escapees' personal belongings at gun point. Escapees would be thrown into jail; there, the Vietcong would gladly help them contact their families for money to bail them out of jail. The Vietcong had many ways to steal from the South Vietnamese and bring them to their knees.

The plan was that two of us would escape first, to a safe destination, and then afterwards, my mother would start her escape with the rest of her children. She had a connection with someone who had relatives living in Hanoi, the capital of North Vietnam. They asked for four ounces of gold to get two of us to Hanoi in a Vietnamese government plane; from Hanoi, they would take us on a train to the Vietnamese border with China. Once at the Vietnamese border with China, our chaperone from Hanoi would leave us to find our own way from China to Hong Kong. Hong Kong meant freedom, as Hong Kong was still a British colony at this time.

One day after school, my sister came home and told my mom about her school situation. She said that the school was brainwashing everyone, telling the students how great the communist party was, referring to the communist party as heroes, and the Americans as bad and evil people. Some of Allison's classmates were leaving the country, one by one. Her class was getting smaller and she asked my mom to find a way out of Vietnam.

We were not safe living in Vietnam, and we did not want to live in Vietnam anymore. Life in Saigon was getting tougher and more desperate by the day. My mother needed to find the safest way for us to escape Vietnam so that we could have a better life and future.

CHAPTER 4

The Unusual Way

This whole escape plan was NOT supposed to be for me. Allison and Warren were supposed to be the first escape group! The day before departure, Warren had a high fever and did not feel well. When the next day arrived, my mother made the decision to have me take Warren's place in the first escape group. I had not been told about the escape plan as it had to be kept secret. This was the moment my life changed: I was about to embark on the most horrific journey of my life.

I was sleeping and dreaming, just like any other child, when my mother woke me up and placed me on a motor bike. She took me to a neighbour's house where she put a communist uniform on me and then sent me to the airport. My poor mom must have been so distraught uncertain of her two adolescent children's fate on this unknown journey, hoping that we would make it out of Vietnam alive.

"Airport?! What am I doing here, at the airport?" I said to myself. No one had told me that I would be leaving home on the run taking a plane from Saigon airport. Finally, my sister said to me, "We are leaving the country." I felt as though we were on holiday, not trying to escape Vietnam, on the run from the communists. Nobody escaped Vietnam by plane it was a very unusual way to leave the country, a wealthy man's way of leaving Vietnam. I thought to myself that my mother must have some kind of connection with a high-ranking North Vietnamese government official.

My sister, Allison, and I boarded an old two-propeller, twin engine plane, headed to Hanoi in North Vietnam. We found ourselves surrounded by Russian soldiers. I thought to myself, "Are we going to a war zone?" I was already very scared and nervous, and this old plane was making me even more nervous and sick. The plane would rise, upend, then dive down. It was non-stop turbulence. I felt like I was riding on a roller coaster for hours. It turned my stomach upside down and my face turned pale I looked like crap when I landed in Hanoi.

The city of Hanoi had been bombed very badly by the American Air Force and the communist government had no money to rebuild. From the plane I could see many shattered buildings and giant potholes.

My sister and I stayed in Hanoi for a few days, waiting for the train to a town called Lao Cai, near the Chinese border. I remember that a lady accompanied us on the train, a guide that my mother had hired to get us to the Chinese border. We took the train at midnight from Hanoi and arrived in Lao Cai at dawn. This was our most exciting moment on our journey thus far.

We were now at the foot of the bridge that would take us across into China, and we waited for its gate to open. We could not wait to cross the bridge and get out of Vietcong hell. As we waited, the lady said to us, "Now that you are both leaving the country, your mom said you should give your jewellery, gold rings, necklaces, watches, and money to me." My sister didn't give her anything, as she knew our mother had not said this.

CHAPTER 5

Entering Deeper into Hell

As soon as the border gate opened, people ran to the bridge. Ignoring the lady, we just picked up our belongings, and crossed the bridge. There were no check-points at either side of the border. We were in the Chinese exodus period, the period when the Vietnamese government permitted ethnic Chinese living in Vietnam to depart Vietnam without questioning.

Many people were carrying their belongings with them: large pieces of luggage, furniture, bicycles even water buffalo! "Why on earth are they bringing animals?" I thought to myself. "This is not an escape. This is like moving to a new country."

We did not fear being stopped or captured by the Vietcong anymore we ran towards China as fast as possible. It was raining and cold. The Chinese border guard lady came toward us to welcome us and help us cross over. She was directing everybody to the temporary refugee camps. We were so glad, and we felt welcomed by the Chinese authorities. We felt safe.

So far we had made it to China with no trouble at all. It was a lot easier than we thought. That was great! We thought, "Are we really out of hell?"

No, we were not. The Chinese communist government did not allow its people to leave the country and thus the Chinese people were not able to tell the Vietnamese people how harsh and oppressive life was in China.

We were on our own, and there was no turning back. We stayed in a refugee camp in China, across the border from Lao Cai, Vietnam, for more than two weeks. All our basic needs, such as water and food, were supplied by the Chinese government. Nobody was starving in the refugee camp. It was a good start to our journey.

Two minors, without a guardian, trying to figure out how we were going to reach our destination Allison and I were totally clueless and naive about how we would get to Hong Kong. Allison tried to make friends with some people who were a lot older than us, asking if we could join them part of the way.

Luckily, we found a family of two brothers and a sister-in-law, the Chong family; they were willing to help us and take us along with them. The Chong family was shocked when they realized that Allison and I were minors travelling alone to China. We were so happy and relieved. During the waiting and planning the weather got really warm, and the blazing sun burned hot on the metal roof of our shelter there were flies and mosquitos everywhere.

CHAPTER 6

My First Near-Death Experience

One day, I followed my sister to the well to do laundry. I was not strong enough to wring and dry the clothes, so I left her and wandered around. I saw a river and decided to explore the surrounding area.

That was the moment that an evil force from hell tried to take away my life. As I was walking along the riverbank, I saw some children screaming and laughing on the other side of the river; they were playing in the water and swimming. It looked like a lot of fun. They got me excited and I could not stand the heat anymore, so I jumped into the river. I thought it would be great to cool off in the water like the other kids. Once I was in the river, I realized that I did not know how to swim. This mistake nearly cost me my life.

I was young and foolish. I had underestimated the force and the depth of the river's current, which swept me away. I was terrified and panicking , I thought for sure that I was going to drown.

I tried to grab the weeds on the riverbank to pull myself back to land, but the grass and the weeds kept breaking off. The river's current was very fast and pulled me under, making me swallow the muddy water. I kept desperately trying to grab whatever I could get my hands onto as I was dragged down the river.

I said to myself: "I'm drowning. Nobody's here to help me. I'm just about to get swept away to the ocean. Oh, God! Please, help me! Help me …" I was about to die.

Luckily, I was able to grab onto a tree root and pull myself up onto the riverbank. I felt that this must have been the hand of God that pulled me out from hell. I was badly shaken when I walked back to the camp, but I did not tell my sister about this brush with death, to avoid getting in trouble.

What would have happened if I had drowned and was swept away, nowhere to be found? My sister and my family would have been very devastated had I disappeared like this, without a trace. This was the first time I came close to death on my journey to freedom.

CHAPTER 7

The Virus Attack

A few days later, I felt sick. I had a headache and a fever, with vomiting and shaking. Allison got me some pills, but they did not work and I became sicker every day. I was laid out on the bed, unable to get up or move.

Our next destination was to be Guangzhou City, in Canton province, near Hong Kong. The day of our departure arrived. My sister, the Chong family, and I packed up all our belongings and walked to the train station very early in the morning. I was barely able to stand up and walk and my sister became really worried about my well-being. She felt helpless, because she could not carry me as well as all our belongings.

She could not believe that this was happening to us everyone was on the move and we could not stay behind alone. This was an unintended difficulty that I created for my sister. I made her feel very frustrated and very worried.

She managed to beg one of the Chong brothers to help us; he dropped his belongings, picked me up, and carried me on his back all the way to the train station a walk of two to three kilometres. It was then that I learned the true extent of people's compassion and kindness.

As we boarded the train, everything seemed smooth, but I was still sick as hell. We were in economy class, and there were no beds to lie on, only chairs. My high fever persisted, and as the time passed by I began shivering. I felt dizzy, cold, and weak. There were no doctors or medicines to help me get better.

CHAPTER 8

The Evil was Tearing Away my Soul

I became weaker and weaker. A quarter of the way to Guangzhou City I finally passed out and fell into a coma I was sitting on my chair, with my head and arm resting on the table attached to the wall, next to my chair. I could not respond to my sister. I believed a virus was destroying me quickly. If my sister did not get me to the hospital soon, I would surely die. I felt that my soul was being torn away by the minute.

I was creating more trouble for my sister, lying there unconscious, with a high-grade temperature, and with no doctor or medication to help me. I must have gotten my sister in a panic she did not know what to do. The Chong family advised my sister to get off the train at the nearest city, which was Kunming City, and put me in the hospital right away.

My poor sister must have been feeling sad and lost. Once we got off the train at Kunming station, she would have to face unexpected and unknown difficulties all by herself. What a terrible trouble-maker I was! Red dots were beginning to show on my face was showing many red dots, indicating that my life was in danger. My eyes were half-open with didn't respond as my sister tried repeatedly to wake me up. My life was running out, minute by minute. Inside, I was crying for help, but no one could hear me. I felt that the Evil One was silently and slowly tearing my soul away from my body! I was in a very desperate situation: if no help arrived soon, I would surely die.

At last the train stop. At Kunming station we separated from the Chong family, who would continue their journey to Guangzhou City. They gave us the address of a relative in Guangzhou City, however, so that we could meet them once I had recovered from my illness. Sadly, for the moment, we were on our own again in a strange place, with no idea of where to get help.

My sister begged an unknown passenger to carry me on his back to the front gate of the train station. Allison left me alone on a bench near the front gate of the train station and walked out, to find someone on the street who could help transport me to the hospital. She found a man who had a small wagon and asked him to carry me to the nearest hospital.

Great job, Allison. Somehow she'd managed it. The hospital that Allison checked me into was a small and run-down building. They were unable to treat my illness there. The staff decided to send me to the central hospital, which was much better. I was unconscious, unaware of how I got to the emergency room. The emergency room doctor gave me some medicine, but I remained unconscious and unresponsive. After many hours the hospital closed, and the hospital staff made Allison leave the hospital.

Allison went outside, feeling helpless, scared, and depressed. She had no place to stay overnight. She wandered about the streets for hours and hours, thinking about how she could possibly afford to pay for my treatment at the hospital, and where she could stay while I was there.

What a disaster I had gotten her into. There were no friends, no family, no neighbours, and no telephone to ask for help. There was absolutely *nothing* available to her. There was nothing that she could do at this time to help me, so she just walked around like a homeless teenager until she got tired. Finally, she sat on a bench and started to cry.

A young man passed by my sister and saw her crying, helplessly. He stopped and asked what the problem was. My sister told him about our situation and that we were not from China. Believe it or not, this young man offered for my sister to stay at his parents' house until I got better. My sister accepted the stranger's offer, as her only other alternative was to sleep on the street. She ended up staying at his house for two days, without any problems. What a daring decision she made. The young man tried to convince Allison to leave me behind and take another escape route to Hong Kong with him. Allison would never leave me behind. Allison refused the young man's offer.

CHAPTER 9

The Good Doctor

Two days passed by, and I regained consciousness. I was able to open my eyes and look at the ceiling and surroundings. Everything was blurry to me and I could not move my hands and legs. I was hooked up to intravenous needles and tied down to my bed. I had tubes all over me. There were four intravenous needles pumping into me at the same time: two on my legs and two on my arms. I must have been seriously ill.

"Oh my God! What kind of mess have I gotten myself into?" I thought. "How did I get into the hospital? I can't remember anything at all."

I tried to get up and see where my sister was, but I could not see her anywhere. I called her name, but she was not around. I could not get up; I was still very weak. A nurse came to comfort me and gave me some medicine. "Your sister is not here. The doctor will come to check on you soon," the nurse said. I lay back on the bed and looked around. No one else was in the room.

Finally, the doctor came to see me. "How are you doing?" he asked. "I don't know," I replied. "I think you are better now," the doctor said. "You were passed out when you were checked in. Now you are awake that is a better sign." Then he asked for my name, my age, and where I lived. Where were my parents? "No one came to see you in the last two days," he said. "Do you remember what happened to you?"

I had no idea what had happened in the past two days. I told the doctor that all I knew was that I was in the train, had a very high fever, and woke up in the hospital. I did not know how and when I got there. The doctor had a lot of questions and concerns about my situation, as nobody had visited me, and I was only thirteen years old.

I was able to communicate with the doctor in Chinese as I come from a Chinese background. I told him we were migrants I had come from Vietnam with my seventeen-year-old sister. We had no guardians with us, no address, and no place to live right now. We were still on the run, and I didn't know what had made me so sick or how I had ended up there.

CHAPTER 10

The Second Near-Death Experience

"You got malaria from mosquito bites. You are very lucky that you made it to the hospital on time and now you are recovering," the doctor said. "Get more rest and wait for your sister to come back. I would like to talk to her."

Thinking back, I could have died if my sister had not put me in the hospital quickly enough. This was the second time I believed that God had pulled me out of hell and spared my young life.

The night passed by, and my sister did not come to see me. This was very frustrating and worrying since there was no way for me to contact her. I was still very ill and had no clue where to find her, so I just lay on the bed and hoped for the best.

The next morning, I still did not see any sign of my sister. The doctor came to my bedside and said, "Nobody has come to see you for two days now. This is not a good sign at all. You have no parents, no place to live, no money, and nobody to care for you. You are such a pitiful little young boy you are suffering, and you would have died if you hadn't made it to the hospital in time. I feel so sorry for you," he said.

He was touching my forehead with his hand when he said this to me: "Would you like to be my adopted son? I will take you in as my own child and I will take care of you and look after you; I don't have any children." I was shocked, and I froze for a moment.

This was a very good offer. I did not get this lucky often. I thought, "The doctor wants to adopt me? Maybe he thinks I was abandoned by my parents. This is a communist country. I definitely don't want to stay here. We're running away from our country to find freedom. I don't think it's a good idea to accept his kindness."

"I don't know, I said. "I'm too young to make this decision. I think it may be better to wait for my sister to come back and we will decide then." It was very kind of him, but still, this was not the place we wanted to stay.

My sister finally showed up the next morning and asked how I was doing. I had gotten much better, but I still had an intravenous line in me. I was not one hundred percent recovered yet. I told my sister that the doctor had asked if I wanted to be adopted by him. She said, "No, I cannot allow that. This is not the place we want to stay for the rest of our lives. We need to find a free country."

CHAPTER 11

No Place for Shelter

"We cannot stay in the hospital any longer. We must leave and go to the train station and continue our journey," she said. "We must rejoin the Chong family. They will help us get to Hong Kong. Can you walk?" she asked. "I think so," I replied. "Good!" she said, "We do not have enough money to pay for the hospital bills, so we have no other choice but to sneak out of the hospital early in the morning when there are not too many nurses around."

I asked my sister where she had been, and she told me the whole story. She explained how, when she had checked me into the hospital, the nurse had told her that I was in a serious condition and must stay, for further examination, but that she had not been allowed to remain at the hospital. She told me about sitting on the bench crying not knowing where to go or where to stay, worried about losing contact with the Chong family who we depended on to get to Hong Kong. She told me about the young man who had helped her by letting her stay at his house. Luckily, this young man did not harm her or take advantage of her.

The next day at dawn, my sister came to the hospital and helped me grab my belongings; we walked out of the hospital, unnoticed. I felt guilty and bad that I had not been able to thank everyone who had saved my life, but I was poor and my situation was urgent. Anyway, in my heart I felt truly grateful for the doctor, the nurses, and the hospital staff who had treated me so well.

We headed to Kunming train station, to catch a train to Guangzhou City to rejoin the Chong family. The train ride was slow and boring. My sister met some Vietnamese refugees on the train. She befriended them and asked them if we could accompany them on their journey to Guangzhou City. They also felt sorry for us, so they were willing to have us travel along with them. This was another stroke of luck for us. It was yet another example of the kindness, compassion, and charity of others that got us through our difficulties in travelling through China to Hong Kong. We discussed with this family where we might find the refugee camp, once we arrived at Guangzhou City, but no one in our travelling group knew anything about it.

At last, we had arrived at Guangzhou City station. It was huge, and this world entirely new to me. Everything in this city was wider, bigger, and there were thousands and thousands of people on the road.

I was shocked by the many noises on the road and the number of bicycles. It looked like an army of ants travelling back and forth. Everybody looked the same. The men and women were all wearing the same type of clothing. Most people were wearing light or dark blue colours and all the women had the same long hair style, with braids or a "half coconut" cut style very strange and very monotonous. All the bicycles also had the same style: "Why is that?" I thought.

We gathered together with the new group of families from the train and started to venture outside of the station. One of the families had a relative in Guangzhou City we asked for directions on how to get to their home. We took a bus, but the bus took us to only the nearest intersection.

Since all of us were tired and hungry, we decided to go into a noodle house to have some lunch before walking to the relative's house. After we placed our food orders, the cashier asked us for food stamps. We looked at each other, each wondering, "What are food stamps?" The restaurant would not sell us any food without food stamps: "The food stamps are from the government, which supplies the people with them every month," the cashier said.

CHAPTER 12

We Became Beggars

We were totally shocked and disappointed. The train staff had not asked us for food stamps for the food they gave us on the train ride. Now how on earth were we going to get food stamps from the government? We were not citizens of China!

This was unbelievable. We asked ourselves where in the world we were, that we could not buy food with money. We had never experienced this kind of food control by the Vietcong. In Vietnam, as long as you had the money, you still could buy as much food as you desired on the black market. This was not the case in China. Everything was strictly controlled by the government. Now, what were we going to eat? We were all starved and thirsty. Where were we going to find food stamps? We all felt very sad and depressed, with a sense of hopelessness.

This was the worst thing we had ever experienced. We had no choice but to beg on the street for our food. We all became beggars.

We spread out along the street, begging people for mercy to spare any food stamps and explaining to them we were refugees from Vietnam and newly-arrived in China.

Eventually, we met some nice people who were willing to give up their limited monthly food stamps for us. We collected enough to buy one bowl of noodles for each of us. We were very happy and excited to fill up our empty stomachs. After lunch, we all continued on our journey to find the relative's house. Finally, we found their house. Luckily, they allowed my sister and me to stay with them overnight, otherwise we would have slept on the street …

We asked the house owner for the whereabouts of the Chong family as we wanted to reunite with them, so they could help us continue our journey to Hong Kong.

CHAPTER 13

Living from House to House

The house looked like an old-fashioned, wealthy mansion. I shared a bed with a boy who was the same age as me. He told me that four families lived in this mansion, with each family living in a corner of it. There was only one washroom outside, which the families had to share. There were around fifteen people living in this mansion, with just one toilet.

I said to the boy, "What if you need to go to the washroom urgently?" "Well, you poop into a plastic bowl and dump it out after," he said. "OK, that would solve the problem," I thought.

After a restful night's sleep we said good-bye and showed our gratitude to the owner and to the family we had travelled with on the train. Then we moved on to find the Chong family. There were no telephones to communicate by, so we just asked a bus driver how to get to the Chong family. Finally, we found them at their relative's house. Their relative lived in a small house a family of three.

My sister and I got lucky again. The relatives of the Chong family let us stay at their house for a few days. They took us out and showed us around the city. This was a crazy adventure for Allison and me: jumping from house to houses that belonged to people who were complete strangers to us. Luckily for us, they were very welcoming strangers.

The city was big and crowded, and full of people and bicycles. Almost everyone dressed the same drab way; they all looked tired, and sad, and angry, with no smiling faces. I felt that they had been suffering unpleasant living conditions under the oppression of the communist regime for many years.

Another surprise came when we were at a shopping centre. We wanted to get things like toothpaste, toothbrushes, face towels, and personal hygiene products. However, the shopkeepers would not sell them to us.

They asked us for personal supply stamps. We were totally shocked again. "What the hell is going on here?" I thought, "Why is it so difficult to buy anything here?" This country's living conditions seemed totally absurd. No wonder the Chinese citizens looked so sad and depressed.

We were saddened and disappointed as we walked back to the house. One of the members of the Chong family asked his relatives about whether they could buy a bicycle to get around instead of taking the bus. Chong's relative said, "It is almost impossible for you to buy one bicycle. The government allows only one bicycle per person, and it would take a full year to get one."

"Why does it take so long to buy one bicycle?" Chong asked. "Well, each month the government will send you one stamp for one part of the bicycle, such as the front wheel. Next month, you will get a stamp for the back wheel; in the next month, a stamp for the frame; then next month, a stamp for the pedals and on and on. So, it will take about one year to collect enough stamps to get a bicycle," Chong's relative said.

This country had absolutely zero freedom. I had never heard of such ridiculous rules and regulations in my life. They were difficult to digest.

CHAPTER 14

It Tastes Very Good

One day, the owner of the house brought some delicacies home for dinner. "What is this meat?" I asked him, "It tastes very good!" He replied, "This is rat, from the countryside. It's OK to eat. They are not city rats. We do not have enough protein stamps for all of you. Country rats are an alternative. We have very little choice." I found the rat meat quite delicious because I was starving for protein. I had not eaten any meat for weeks.

That was my first rat-meat experience. Eat what you get, I guess. We were very lucky to meet the Chong family and their relatives as they treated us like family. We stayed in that house for a few days, and then the owner of the house mentioned to us that a government refugee camp had recently opened in town. This was good news for my sister and me as we would not have to keep on sleeping at different strangers' houses.

It was time to move on, so we thanked Chong's relatives for taking such good care of us over those last few days. Chong's family, my sister, and I moved to the government refugee camp in Guangzhou City and stayed there for a few weeks. The government refugee camp supplied refugees with basic daily food needs and other basic necessities of life. As a result, we felt relieved and much better. The Chinese government had not yet decided what to do with the refugees living in this refugee camp. They had not yet decided where to settle these refugees from Vietnam.

The good thing was that we did not get locked up. We were roaming the city freely, travelling in and out of the camp. We went out one evening to a night market looking for a night snack. I knew how to read Chinese, due to my Chinese ethic background. I looked at the menu on the wall and was shocked. It said, "Herbals soup with cat meat and penguin meat?" Wow! They truly had run out of meat! We did not dare to try it. I had already tried the rat meat, and I did not think I could try the cat meat. We ate something normal instead.

My sister Allison tried to send a letter home to my mom to let her know that we were still alive in China, but she was not able to. However, she was able to send a letter to our cousin in Hong Kong. We hoped our cousin could pass the news about my sister and me to our mother. I really missed my mom and my brothers and my sister back in Vietnam. I had left them in a flash about one month before. I was a dire situation. My sister and I were worried about our family back home. We did not know how they were keeping, and my mother did not know whether Allison and I were dead or alive.

CHAPTER 15

Demonstration Gone Wrong

Every morning inside the refugee camp, we met and gathered with other refugees to find out how to get to Hong Kong. Once we got to Hong Kong, we would be free to travel to North America. Some of the refugees who had come to the refugee camp earlier than us had found a way to get to the Hong Kong-China border by train. However, when they arrived at the border they had been denied entry into Hong Kong by the Hong Kong government. According to Hong Kong's refugee policy, any refugees from Vietnam who had entered China *before* entering Hong Kong were denied entry. Hong Kong was a British colony at the time.

Hong Kong would only accept refugees who came by water! This was totally devastating for us. After we had gone through all these travelling nightmares, our dream of freedom was shattered.

We could not understand it. We were only migrating through China. We had no intention of staying there. We had left Vietnam for freedom, not for harsher and more oppressive communist living conditions. There was very little freedom to even buy the simple, basic staples we needed. This country's living conditions were horrible. It was like living in jail, without being physically locked up in a cell.

My sister met a young man in the refugee camp, whose name was Minh (my future brother in-law). Minh courted her. He was about twenty-five years old, and had come to China from Vietnam by himself. My sister needed to find someone to trust and depend on, to help us get out of China.

Day after day passed, and more and more refugees poured into the refugee camp. As a result, our living conditions in the camp became increasingly tighter, and the refugees became increasingly frustrated from not being able to cross the border into Hong Kong. The refugees decided to organize a street demonstration protesting the fact that they could not enter Hong Kong. They held posters and signs, and shouted, "We want freedom, we want freedom," as they marched in the direction of the hotel full of foreign tourists, located near our camp.

CHAPTER 16

The Military Takes Action

We wanted to send a message to the outside world that we needed help. We needed the United Nations and the Red Cross to help us get out of China and into a free country. The demonstration was an embarrassment to the Chinese Communist Party as it made them appear to be taking poor care of the refugees from Vietnam. The police did not like the demonstration at all. Nobody had dared to demonstrate like this in China for the last forty years.

The Vietnamese refugees from our camp caused a shock wave across the city, as they shouted for help and freedom in public places and in politically-sensitive places. This first demonstration scared the Chinese Communist Party. They feared it could inspire Chinese citizens to join similar demonstrations and thus trigger an uprising. The Chinese police loathed the demonstration.

After the first demonstration, the refugees went back to the camp and started planning for a second demonstration hoping one of the foreign guests at the hotel would spread our message to the outside world. There were no foreign aid organizations in China that the refugees could reach out to for help absolutely none. The Vietnamese refugees were hoping the demonstration would soon bring hope and help from the democratic and free world. We were all tired and fed up with the harsh living conditions in China. Living in the refugee camp for the past two months had not been a good experience, to say the least. We were constantly guarding our belongings.

As the sun went down, the refugees went back to their rooms to chat, and exchange ideas and information in order to plan the next protest against the British government for not allowing us to enter Hong Kong.

The next day, the refugees started their demonstration again in the same area. However, the Chinese communists did not want us to continue carrying out these demonstrations. They had already preparations in place. The police waited for all the refugees to come back to the camp after this second demonstration, and then took action at midnight, while the refugees were sleeping.

The Chinese military and the police stormed into the refugee camp buildings and started shouting, "Get up! All of you! and get out of the building! Now!" The police and military woke everyone up and dragged people out of their rooms with their belongings. All the refugees were shocked and confused thrown into a panic.

CHAPTER 17

The Labour Camp

"What is going on? What are you people doing? Why are you taking our belongings?" the refugees cried out. "Get up and get out of this building. All of you are leaving this building and getting on the truck!" the police shouted. "Where are you taking us?" "We will let you know when you get there! Move your butts or we will drag you out."

Obviously, none of the refugees wanted to move, because we were not sure where they were going to take us. The police dragged everyone out and tossed them into military trucks.

We were separated from the Chong family and Minh, my sister's boyfriend, in the chaos. Now my sister and I were back to square one, on our own again. The people that my sister and I had been depending on had disappeared.

We were very afraid, not knowing where we would end up. It was dark and we were unsure what they were going to do to us. We did not know anyone on the truck. But at least we were all from Saigon. It was a long, rough, and nerve-racking ride. There were no streetlights and no houses. At last, the truck stopped. The sun had risen by this time and the military and police personnel told us to get out of the truck. They handed us over to the village superintendent.

The superintendent divided four families into groups and put us in houses. There were six houses in a row. Each house had four wooden bed frames with no mattresses, no pillows, and no blankets. There was no toilet, no kitchen, and no table; there were no chairs, either. For water, we had to go to the well. The only light in the house was a small ceiling light. It looked like a labour camp for prisoners.

We soon discovered that we'd been placed into a tea camp. After we settled down in the house, the superintendent, Mr. Lee, gathered everyone for a brief meeting. He provided each family with a clay stove, two pots, some rice bowls, and utensils. The only food we were given were some vegetables and rice. Protein would be delivered by the government once a week frozen pork liver or canned fish.

"All the adults must come to the tea field and pick tea leaves every day," Mr. Lee told us. "Each person must pick several kilograms per day to earn enough money for their daily needs." The children were not required to work, but there were no schools in the camp.

CHAPTER 18

The American Children

The next morning, we introduced ourselves to each other. We all felt relieved that we hadn't been locked up. I was surprised to see four Americans in the camp with us; three of them had blonde hair and white skin. This first American family (there were two) had two girls and one boy, all of whom were much older than me perhaps eighteen to twenty years old. They were very good-looking and very tall. Their father, Mr. Trang, was ethnic Chinese but was escaping from his life in Vietnam, just like me. Mr. Trang was somewhere in his mid-fifties. He looked like a businessman as he always wore a white shirt, black pants, and black leather shoes. He was not travelling with a wife or companion, only with his three adopted, adult, American children who looked quite different from each other, so I assumed they had come from different families. Mr. Trang's children spoke the same languages as me: Chinese and Vietnamese. They didn't speak English, just like me.

The second American family in the camp had a smaller girl, who had dark black hair and looked about the same age as me (about twelve years old). She was with her grandmother and a younger sister. She looked more like a French and Vietnamese mix, and she was very pretty.

There was a total of eight families in this camp. A few single young men and women shared the same house with us. Each morning the adults in the camp followed the local Chinese young men and women to the tea field to pick tea leaves. There was not much to eat. There was no market, no store, and no bus service. There was not even a bicycle. Our only mode of transportation was our two legs.

My sister met a young local Chinese woman at the tea field, and they became friends. This lady was very friendly. She showed us how to survive with almost nothing to live on. She taught us to pick the dried pine cones to make fire for cooking food, as we did not have any tools to chop down trees for firewood. We had never lived on a farm before in our lives. She showed us where to find fresh vegetables from local farmers and how to walk through farm fields to buy vegetables and fruit at the local farmers' market.

This market opened only once a week, on Saturday mornings. There was no road to get there from our tea camp instead, a miserable three-hour muddy walk across fields, coming back to the tea camp carrying food staples in our hands. It was the only place we could buy protein such as eggs and beans and the only place we could buy cooking oil, salt, pepper, sugar, and other spices without government food stamps.

CHAPTER 19

Wasteful Young Chinese Lives

I missed everything from back home in Saigon. I missed ice cream, cookies, candies, noodles, toys, games. I had absolutely nothing for amusement.

The only thing that kept me company was a little puppy that belonged to the tea camp superintendent. I called the puppy Dory. He was very cute. Dory liked me because I was the only person in the camp who would play with him. Dory came to see me every morning, wanting me to pet him. We became good friends, and the only friend that I adored.

A few weeks went by. Some families left the tea camp, to find their way back to Guangzhou City, where they would try to get to Hong Kong by boat. Unfortunately, my sister and I did not have much money. As a result, we just hung out with the local young Chinese men and women who lived in the camp with us.

They were all from different Chinese provinces. We were curious about these young Chinese who had lived in the tea camp for many years. Why had they lived there for so long? They told us that they had no choice. The government had no work for them in the city. If they didn't work in the city, they would not get food stamps or lodging. During this time, all Chinese citizens living in China were under the Chinese communist government housing program; under this program, there were not enough houses in the cities for all Chinese citizens to live in and thus some Chinese had to live camps, like the tea camp that we were currently staying in.

Since the beginning of the Chinese Communist Revolution in 1949, all of the wealth, land, businesses, property, and almost everything else owned by Chinese citizens was confiscated by the Chinese Communist Party. Wealthy families had to flee the country or face either imprisonment or the death penalty. It was a crime for anyone to own a business and to hire employees; it was *not* a crime when the Chinese communist regime robbed all of the Chinese citizens' wealth and land at gunpoint.

The young Chinese men and women living in the tea camp got to see their family only once a year, during the new year holiday. There was no time limit for how long they would have to stay in this terrible, lifeless camp. Their future was totally destroyed by government regulations. They had no opportunities to train for a vocation or a career. All they did was pick tea leaves all day long, with no other activities at all. They all felt very frustrated and that they were wasting their talents and their lives.

Day by day, my sister was getting progressively more nervous and depressed. She was having difficulty getting in touch with family and friends, in order to get their help to get us out of the tea camp.

CHAPTER 20

Reaching for Support

My sister tried to locate Minh, who had been separated from us when we were removed from our last refugee camp in Guangzhou City. My sister sent a letter to one of Minh's relatives in Hong Kong, hoping to find out where Minh was. In the letter she gave Minh's relative our present location.

Finally, we were able to locate Minh, but it took a while. My sister told him that we had been in this tea camp for a few months now and that a lot of the families from our refugee group had already left the camp. These other families had hired a boat to sail to Hong Kong, as Hong Kong would only accept refugees from Vietnam arriving by water, not from mainland China. The house that we were staying at in was now pretty empty my sister and I were the only two people remaining. Also, most of the houses in the tea camp that had been filled up with Vietnamese refugees were now empty, except for a few young adult Vietnamese refugees and Mr. Trang and his three children.

My sister had also sent letters to our cousin in Hong Kong, asking him to support us with some money so we could pay for our boat fare to Hong Kong. (Mr. Trang was organizing the boat.) Sure enough, we received good news from our cousin: he was willing to send us money. He made an arrangement to have one of his friends bring us the money, when his friend was on holiday in Guangzhou City.

This was a relief and great news for my sister and me. We were very happy and excited. We had great hopes of being able to leave this hell. My sister asked someone in the tea camp to look after me, while she travelled to Guangzhou City to meet our cousin's friend and get the money for the boat fare.

While my sister was away, I got to play with my little puppy friend, Dory. We played with each other every day, from morning to night, and we were always very happy to see each other. We were inseparable. We would run, play, and laugh together. I could see him grow, day by day. This was the best time ever for me during this miserable journey, but it wouldn't last much longer …

CHAPTER 21

The Shattered Moment

One day, Dory and I were sitting under a tree when the superintendent came along, with a smile on his drunken face. Without saying a word, he pulled Dory out of my lap and whacked the puppy's head with a big wooden stick. I was in shock. I could not believe my eyes. I couldn't believe what I was seeing! I stood up and started screaming at the superintendent at the top of my lungs. "What are you doing? Why are you hitting the puppy?!" My poor puppy was in serious pain; he was yelping and whimpering, and blood was gushing from his head. I was in a state of panic and desperate to save Dory.

The superintendent proceeded to wrap a rope around Dory's neck and began strangling him. I tried to jump in to save Dory, but was pushed way by the evil superintendent; he was much bigger than me. Dory continued yelping and twisting his body. The puppy's blood was splashing everywhere all over my body and all over the superintendent's body. Then the superintendent hung poor Dory from a tree branch, causing him to suffocate to death.

I was in tears and begging the superintendent to have mercy on Dory and let him go free. He looked at me with a devilish smile and said, "This is my dog and I am going to eat it for my dinner tonight. So, beat it." He laughed.

I was in shock, helpless, as my best friend died, brutally, in front of my eyes. He was the only friend I had. The joyful moments I had experienced with my best friend Dory were shattered. I felt as though I had lost a family member. My heart was broken. I was kneeling down, crying over Dory's barely-alive body. I felt horrible, because I was incapable of saving Dory; all I could do was stand by helplessly, as the superintendent killed him. I kept asking myself, "Why did the superintendent have to kill the puppy for food? Why ?!"

The evil superintendent took the lifeless puppy away into his kitchen. My happy moments with the puppy were brief, and now my best friend was gone forever, in a bloody, brutal, and horrific way. I was angry because there was no one else for me to play with and to talk with. I was back in hell, with more nightmares on the way!

CHAPTER 22

The Endless Nightmare

My sad days passed by in the tea camp, and my sister returned, looking disappointed. "What's going on?" I asked. "I did not get the money," she replied. "What? What happened?"

She told me that when she had arrived at the hotel where our cousin's friend was staying, he had locked her into his hotel room, undressed himself, and attempted to rape her. She had pushed him away and had run into the bathroom and locked herself in desperately thinking how she would get out of this dangerous situation. Unfortunately, there were no windows in the bathroom for her to escape by. She had yelled out to him from the washroom, asking him to get her water from the fridge. As our cousin's friend had walked, totally naked, to the fridge, Allison had taken a chance running out of the bathroom as fast as she could, unlocking the suite's door, and making a run for the hotel lobby.

Her daring escape had worked. She had managed to escape being raped by this monster. She ran for her life, crying out, down the hotel's hallway and out of the hotel, without any of our cousin's money. The mission had gone terribly wrong. What was happening to us? What did we do wrong? Why were we being punished? Why?!

My first punishment was that I nearly drowned.

My second punishment was that I got so sick and almost died from malaria, putting my sister in harm's way in Kunming City by making her stay in a stranger's house because she was not allowed to stay in Kunming City Hospital. When we got to Guangzhou City we had to continuously move from one stranger's house to another's.

My third punishment was when we moved into the refugee camp in Guangzhou City, which we were later forcibly removed from by the Chinese police due to the demonstrations for freedom. As a result, we were re-located to the tea camp that we were currently living in, with barely enough food to keep us alive.

My fourth punishment was when my friend Dory, the only best friend I'd ever had, was slaughtered and eaten by his owner, in front of my eyes.

The fifth punishment occurred when my sister almost got raped by our cousin's friend and wasn't able to get the money we needed so desperately in order to get out of China. Now we were in complete despair as we had no money to pay for the boat fare. We couldn't take any more punishment.

Allison and I hugged each other, crying in an empty, cold house with no one to care for us. All the sorrow we felt, however, could not destroy our dream of freedom. We knew that we had to stay strong and persevere in order to overcome challenges on this journey. We wouldn't give up! We were determined to reach our place of freedom!

CHAPTER 23

No Alternative

On the bright side, my sister felt glad and fortunate that she had managed to escape from our cousin's friend. We were so vulnerable and fragile at this time. Bad experiences seemed to follow us, and there seemed to be no end in sight to our bad luck. We did not know what was coming next …

After my sister came back from Guangzhou City empty-handed, she knew she had to act fast to find another source of help for us. She turned to Minh for help. She asked him to come to our tea camp and join us on our plan to take a boat to Hong Kong. Minh came, but he was also in a tough situation. Minh tried to get financial help from his relatives in Hong Kong, but it wasn't enough to pay for the boat fare for all three of us.

Mr. Trang had organized a boat to get us all to Hong Kong and had asked everyone in the tea camp to pay a fixed fee in order to get on the boat. We became increasingly worried and panicked as we still did not have enough money to pay the boat fare. What if

Mr. Trang were to leave without us? There wouldn't be anyone else left in the camp who could help us to get out of China.

This was an opportunity, possibly our last, to get to Hong Kong. We couldn't afford to lose it. So, my sister went to Mr. Trang and gave him all the money we had her necklace and her jade pendant. She explained that we did not have any guardians to take care of us and that she almost got raped in Guangzhou City by our cousin's friend. Thankfully, Mr. Trang was merciful, and allowed us to join him for the boat journey to Hong Kong.

My sister, however, was not able to avoid being raped, after all. Minh stayed with us in the house that we had shared with other families when we had first arrived at the camp. Now, however, only my sister and I remained. In the middle of the night, Minh sneaked into Allison's bed and demanded to have sex with her.

Allison was still a virgin. She did not want to have sex with Minh. But she had no choice but to obey him, because we needed his financial help. What a horrible thing to have happened to her! She thought she had gotten away from being raped, but now she was being raped by Minh. She wasn't in love with him; she was only seventeen years old, and had never even dated. She said to herself that if she tried to resist Minh's sexual advances, we would stay in this camp forever. There wouldn't be a second chance to leave China.

Minh took advantage of her; he forced himself on Allison without her consent. From then on, Minh demanded sex from Allison whenever he felt like it.

Allison became depressed and felt lost and confused afraid that she would become pregnant with the unprotected sex, that her dreams and ambitions would be shattered. I feel guilty and sad about what she endured and sacrificed to get us out of hell. Nevertheless, I'm so proud of her.

CHAPTER 24

The Sea Journey

This journey was much too difficult and dangerous for us to handle. We were young and inexperienced, but we were in the middle of it, and had to find a way out of it somehow. Otherwise, we knew for certain we would be doomed.

Mr. Trang had bought a junk boat (a Chinese sailing boat) near Hainan Island a Chinese island near the south coast of China, east of Vietnam.

The plan was that our boat-travelling group my sister, Minh, myself, Mr. Trang and his family, and a few young Vietnamese men and women refugees from the tea camp would travel by train to a town near Hainan Island, and join up with another group of Vietnamese refugees.

We would set sail along the shoreline of Hainan Island all the way to Hong Kong. We felt so happy and excited that Mr. Trang had decided to help us get to Hong Kong on his boat; this feeling of relief was a great contrast to the fear and worry we had been living with so far on this journey.

CHAPTER 25

The Pig Barn

A few days before sailing, the adults stocked up with supplies such as dried foods, water, rice, and chopped wood for cooking. There were no portable gas stove or portable electric burner at that time.

We were unable to buy protein in China without government-issued protein food stamps, as protein was supplied solely by the government. We decided, nonetheless, to take a risk in order to try to get protein for our boat trip to Hong Kong. If caught, it could result in harsh punishment by the Chinese authorities. The risk was this: to steal a pig from the government pig barn near our house in the tea camp. We did not have a choice, we all needed some protein to survive our journey. This made the boat trip a one-way ticket if we failed, and had to return to the tea camp, we would be severely punished by superintendent for stealing.

The safest time to steal a pig was during the day, when all the people in the tea camp were working in the field. And so, when everyone else was away working, we went into the pig barn where there were fifty to sixty pigs and we picked the smallest one.

We slaughtered the pig, cut it into long, thin strips, and cured it with sea salt. We then tied rope to the pig meat and hung it up at the front of the house to sun-dry it for a few days. But we brought the pig meat back inside the house when the camp workers came back from working in the tea field, so they would not see it. Two days had gone by and no one had discovered the missing pig. We were very nervous. By the third day after stealing the pig we were all packed up. We left the camp when the other camp residents were working in the tea field.

Mr. Trang had arranged for three farm wagons from the local farmer to pick us up and take us to the bus station. Feelings of anxiety and uncertainty about the boat journey were built up, as we travelled to the bus station. There was no Plan B, and there was no turning back. We felt like a group of homeless animals, migrating from place to place, struggling to keep ourselves alive. There would be no way of communicating with each other if we ever became separated.

CHAPTER 26

The Chinese Junk Boat

After travelling for many hours on buses and trains we finally arrived at the small town of Xiu Cheng, near Hainan Island, where we would board our boat to Hong Kong. The boat that we were boarding was commonly referred to as a "Chinese Junk Boat." It was about twenty-four feet long and about twelve feet wide. Our Chinese junk boat looked very old and like it was in terrible condition it was worn out and falling apart. It didn't have a motor and it only had one sailing mast. Unfortunately, we did not have enough money to buy a better boat.

We stayed inside the junk boat for two nights, waiting for more supplies and for the other group of Vietnamese refugees. Altogether, our party consisted of twenty-five people. This meant very tight travelling conditions. Despite the poor condition of the boat and the fact that it was overloaded with people and weight, we still felt very excited; a sense of freedom was being born within us, and we began to have hope for a better life.

By early morning we had begun our boat ride to freedom. It started smoothly. Everyone onboard was very happy and excited. Some shared stories of their journey so far. Others played the guitar and sang, to keep their spirits up. The boat journey would take four to five days.

The first day of sailing went well. The boat was moving fast as the wind was very strong. However, during the evening, a storm began, causing the tide to get rougher and us to slow down. Dark clouds were moving in. A big storm was about to hit the area, although the boat's captain had had no notification of the impending storm. To make a bad situation worse, we were sailing with little preparation, and no experience or knowledge of this route to Hong Kong. There was no safety equipment no radio transmitters, no flares, and no life jackets. We had only a few rubber tubes, one on each side of the boat.

By late evening, our worst nightmare came true: the rain started falling, the wind got stronger, and the waves got rougher. The rain was falling harder and harder. The sound of thunder was roaring very loudly, and lightning bolts were striking in every direction. Inside the boat, everyone became afraid. The boat was rocking from side to side and waves were smashing and pounding it.

The captain shouted at the sailors young men from our group, they had never sailed a boat in their lives to change the boat's direction so that the waves would not hit the side of the boat, and destroy or capsize it.

CHAPTER 27

Violent Storm

There were no seats, there was just an empty space in the belly of the boat. We all sat on the floor of the belly of the boat and held onto each other tightly, eyes closed, praying for the boat not to break apart. The storm did not slow down, and we were in the middle of a violent sea. The waves were tossing the sail boat around like a toy.

People inside the boat were also being tossed around as there was nothing to hang on to. Water was gushing into the belly of the boat and everyone got drenched. The waves kept on slamming into the boat and each time more water would come gushing in. People were soaking wet and rolling around like dice. Sea water flooded the floor of the boat. Everyone was panicking. Everyone was scrambling to hold onto the wall. Our luggage floated in the pool of water in the belly of the boat.

The captain noticed that the boat was tilting to one side. If our boat stayed in this position much longer it would capsize easily. The captain shouted for some of the people to move to the other side of the boat, to keep it from capsizing. I prayed that the boat would stay intact. The storm was way too big for this piece of junk to handle! The squeaking sound of the frame of the boat was terrifying. The horror on everyone's face was indescribable.

The storm became more violent; the waves got even bigger and pounded the boat heavily. The captain shouted to the sailors to let the sail down, to avoid having it rip apart. The sea was so rough that it made it very difficult for the young men to keep their balance on the top deck they could easily fall off the boat, into the sea.

All of a sudden, we heard a big bang. The pole that held the boat's sail had broken off and fallen into the sea. We were going down. We had lost both our sail and our sail pole. We were not sailing anywhere, and this violent storm was going to smash the boat into pieces.

I was scared as hell. I could not find my sister because there were no lights inside the boat, and it was the middle of the night. Anything that could give light, such as our oil lantern, was wet and ruined. I managed to claw my way to the front window of the boat to see what was going on outside. The waves in front of me were enormous. I estimated that they were about five storeys high. One of these five-storey waves slammed right onto the window where I was standing.

CHAPTER 28

Castaway

The wave was like a giant wall of water. It was bigger than my eyes could see. I froze as I saw it rising up so high. It smashed so hard onto the front of the boat that it burst through the window and violently pushed me to the back of the boat.

The wave knocked me right out. I was unconscious, and my body floated like a dead fish in the large pool of water in the belly of the boat. This moment felt as though all of hell's demons were trying to pull my soul down to hell. I did not know what was happening to the other people on the boat, nor what was happening to the boat itself.

If our junk boat had broken in half, I would surely have died, as I was completely unconscious and thus totally incapable of saving myself from drowning. When I finally came to, there was something very bright shining into my eyes. As I regained my consciousness, everything around me was very quiet. I was lying on my back on the floor and was thinking to myself, "Am I still alive? Am I dreaming?" I turned my head and saw that almost everyone else was lying down, with their eyes closed, motionless on the floor.

Nothing was moving and our junk boat was very still. I got up and ran to the upper deck to see what was happening. As I looked at the sea from the boat's upper deck, I saw a vast mirror surrounding us. "What is going on?" I asked myself. The sea was so calm that I could see my reflection in the water. There was no wind, no waves, no birds, no sounds, and nobody was talking.

I turned to a sailor, who was sitting motionless nearby, and asked, "What is going on? Why are we not moving?" The sailor replied, "The pole that holds our only sail and the steering stick of the boat are both broken."

I had survived, once again. In fact, it was miraculous that we all survived this storm in the middle of the sea. The battle with the storm was over, and we had survived …!

CHAPTER 29

Drifting Aimlessly at Sea

But it was not over yet. Sailing to our destination was now hopeless. We were going nowhere, drifting aimlessly in the vast South China sea. Everyone on the boat looked tired and disappointed. There were no passing boats. We did not have a flare gun to signal for help. We could not send a smoke signal because everything had been soaked by the storm. We had no wood to cook food with, and nothing around us but sea water. The only thing left for all of us to share was a few, small water bottles.

The captain advised everyone to take turns to look out for any boats passing by. This was the most helpless and hopeless moment of our entire journey thus far. We certainly did not want to starve to death in the middle of the sea.

Our boat drifted all day and all night. No boats came by, but we were still hopeful that we would be rescued.

The boat was being pushed by the slow-moving waves. At night I looked up at the sky and saw what looked to be millions and millions of stars. The moon looked exceptionally bright, illuminating the night sky and the sea around us. It was beautiful and so tranquil. I heard nothing, except for the sound of the waves. Sadly, though, the beautiful scenery of the sky did not make any of us feel any better about our situation.

I still could not believe our junky-looking boat had survived the storm; however, it was badly damaged. We all went to sleep early, to recharge despite being in our wet clothes and lying on wet pillows. The night went by smoothly. All of a sudden, we heard a big bang and felt our boat tilting to one side.

The bang woke everybody up and people were screaming. "We are hit! Did we just hit something?!" people shouted. It sent us into another wave of panic. I pulled myself up off the floor of the boat and crawled to the window to see what had happened.

Our boat had, in fact, hit land in the early morning hours. I could see a beautiful beach. I was so excited I jumped off the boat and onto the beach where our boat had come ashore. I was so happy to feel land beneath my feet on this pristine sandy beach.

CHAPTER 30

The Robinson Family

We were back on land; I could not wait to find something to eat and drink. Everyone spread out to explore the land and find help. We were hoping for some good luck.

We discovered that we had landed on a tiny island in the middle of the South China Sea. There was nothing on this island. No! It had only a rocky hill with some trees just an isolated, little island. It did not have any houses, nor did it have any people. If we had been on the mainland, we would have been able to find people to help us, save us. Now that we had landed on a desolate island, there was nobody who could help us. We were back in the jaws of hell again.

We were castaways, like the Robinson family from the television series *The Robinson Family*. They were much better off than us as though they had tools to build shelters for protect themselves from the elements, and they had coconut trees to supply them with coconuts for drinking water and food to keep them alive. We had nothing to eat and nothing to drink. Everything had been soaked, so we couldn't cook any of our pork or rice. We would not have dared to eat them uncooked, as we knew very well the risk of illness and possible death.

Our experience thus far could be described as disappointment after disappointment, desperate moment after desperate moment, disaster after disaster, horrific experience after horrific experience, anxiety after anxiety, fear after fear, panic after panic, failure after failure, risk after risk. We were in a constant state of distress! We had survived an ocean storm, but there were many obstacles to our freedom that still lay ahead.

As we could not find any food, water, or people on the island, we went back to our broken junk boat. We retrieved our belongings and brought them out onto land so they could dry. We hoped that our matches, lighters, and wood once they, too, had dried might make a fire for cooking.

CHAPTER 31

Digging our Graves

I found a little bit of drinkable water, dripping from the rocks of the hill. It relieved my thirst. Sadly, though, there were no fruit trees or edible vegetation on the island.

What were the chances that a boat would pass by? We kept our spirits up and hoped for some good luck! Again, the captain asked everyone take turns watching out for passing ships.

I explored the beach, picking up rocks, hoping to find seafood such as shellfish and sure enough, I found some baby crabs. This would be a treat for my hungry stomach! But then I realized that we weren't able to make a fire to cook the crabs. Since I did not want to get sick in the middle of this desolate island, I gave up my plan to eat the crabs and decided to go swimming instead.

Our boat was lying on the beach, tilted on its side. Since there was not enough space on the boat for everyone to sleep inside, my sister, Minh, and I decided to sleep on the beach by the hill. There were a lot of mosquitos at night, and we did not have any mosquito nets with us. Minh had brought some plastic sheets with him, just in case we needed to sleep on the street on our journey to Hong Kong. Unfortunately, they were not big enough to make a tent, but my sister and Minh came up with an idea. With a cooking pot they dug a shallow grave and used some of Minh's plastic sheets to cover the bottom of the grave the remaining plastic sheets covered the top of the grave. Then they placed some small rocks and along the perimeter of the top plastic sheet, so that the wind wouldn't blow it away. This idea worked, as it protected us from the mosquitos and sheltered us from the rain.

It was dark and cold at night. We were very hungry but there was no cooked food available. We were exhausted from the storm, and the shipwreck and had no difficulty falling asleep. We slept very well through the night, without any interruptions it was extremely quiet, since we were in the middle of nowhere!

CHAPTER 32

The Chinese Fisherman

Early in the morning we heard someone from our boat shouting, "Help! Help! Help! Help!" We jumped out of our grave and checked what was going on. There was a small boat passing by the island! Everyone who was sleeping on our junk boat immediately jumped out and started waving and shouting for help. I ran quickly to the ocean, jumping up and down and shouting at the top of my lungs. This was a very exciting moment. We were hopeful that this boat would stop and rescue us. We believed it was the only chance we had to be rescued.

The boat was a small fishing boat from China, about six-foot long, and I estimated that it could hold only about four people. The boat acknowledged us and slowed down to check on us. Someone had found us here on this deserted island!

All the adults ran toward the man, who swam to us from his fishing boat, and helped him to the shore. He looked at all of us. He could tell that we were not from China, as Mr. Trang's children looked white. We told him that we were all ethnic Chinese from

Vietnam and that we were trying to get to Hong Kong. We told him that our junk boat had been damaged by the storm two days ago and that we had not eaten since then. We desperately needed his help.

The man walked over to our boat to see what was broken. "Well, first things first. I have to bring you people some water and food from my house. Then, I will check out the broken parts of the junk boat and see where there is a shipyard that can fix it," he said.

"You are a wonderful man. Our lives depend on you. Thank you so much for helping us," Mr. Trang said. The man swam back to his boat and we waved at him hoping, with a little scepticism, that he would come back to help us out.

Unfortunately, the man did not have any spare food on his boat to give us today, so we went hungry for another day. We kept looking out at the ocean, hoping another boat would pass by to rescue us. All we could do was comfort each other and hope for better luck.

Hour by hour, wave by wave, the ocean water pushed higher and higher up the beach, but there were no signs of any more ships. Then the sun finally set. It was time to get back to our grave and go hungry for another night.

CHAPTER 33

The Hippy Shirt Deal

While we were sleeping, there was a honking sound. Wow! That sounds like a boat honking at us! Again, we ran to the ocean and saw the same boat from the day before. We were so happy and rushed to his boat to see what he had got for us. The man had baked us a huge sponge cake. We were very excited to have our stomachs filled. We were so hungry, that we grabbed the cake with our bare hands and stuffed it right into our mouths.

We were eating like cavemen. Oh, my Lord! It was a very simple cake, but still the best cake ever. We thanked the man a million times for coming back to help us. "I don't have any protein to bring to you all, because I don't have enough for myself, and this cake is the only thing I can spare to help you out," the man said.

He also brought us some wood and matches, which could keep us alive for a few more days. The man told us he could not find any shop that made the parts that were necessary to get the junk boat sailing again. He said he would try to find the broken parts at a shop in another village the following day.

Mr. Trang offered the fisherman some U.S. money to pay for the sponge cake and supplies. The man refused, saying, "I can not accept this type of currency. If the local police catch me with it, they will throw me in jail for holding U.S. dollars."

"Wow! OK. What can we offer you?" Mr. Trang asked. The man was looking at Mr. Trang's white children and pointed at Mr. Trang's daughter's flowery hippy shirt. "The flower shirt is very colourful and beautiful. Maybe we can trade it, in exchange for the sponge cake and supplies? My wife would be very happy to have that. We cannot buy these clothes in the shop," the fisherman said. "Alright, we certainly will trade this flowery shirt with you," Mr. Trang.

That trade was a shock to us. We could not believe a used hippy shirt could save us from starvation. Some things we would never have thought. It was great. We got some food and help from this nice fisherman who came out of nowhere. This was a very good sign to all of us, but we were still praying that the replacement part would come for our junk boat so we could continue sailing to Hong Kong.

The very next morning, the man came back from the sea and brought us some fish that he had caught. This was very kind of him. Unfortunately, the replacement part for our junk boat never came. There were no shipyards near our island that carried the replacement part. This was extremely disappointing. The only thing left that he could do to help us was to let the local police know about our situation, so that they could come to take us off the island. However, we felt very uncomfortable contacting the local police because we did not want them to take us to another labour camp in China. Sadly, he could not do anything else to help us, such as towing our boat to Hong Kong with his boat. Since he was a Chinese citizen, the Hong Kong government would not allow him to enter Hong Kong territory.

CHAPTER 34

Must be God's Creation

Mr. Trang had to make a crucial decision soon; we had been stranded on this island for three days now, and we were going nowhere. We refused to get the local police involved, so we decided to wait for the kind fisherman to find another boat to pull us to the Chinese mainland.

After the fisherman left us, we returned to standing at lookout, watching out for rescue boats. It was a very foggy day, when what appeared to be a tiny light-blue boat emerged slowly out of the thick ocean fog. It was like something out of a movie.

We heard the sound of a running motor, and we got very excited again! We waved to the boat and shouted for help. The tiny blue boat slowed down and checked us out. In the boat was a man, a woman, and two small children. The man jumped off the boat and started walking towards us. We spoke to him in Chinese, asking for help, but he did not understand us. We heard his wife shout to him in Vietnamese, "Be careful!" We got more excited. Mr. Trang shouted to him in Vietnamese, "Help us, my dear Vietnamese brother." Oh, my God. We could not believe this! They were refugees from Vietnam, also journeying to Hong Kong. Somehow, they had got lost and ended up passing by this remote island.

They had no clue how they had got to here. They were lost. This must have been God's plan. It was an unbelievable coincidence, a miracle. It was totally surreal, like something you would see only in a movie. But, fortunately for us, this was not a movie; it was our reality! We knew this was a golden opportunity for us to get off the island an opportunity that we could not let slip away. This was our only chance to survive and get to Hong Kong for freedom.

"You don't know how glad we are to see you!" the captain of our junk boat said to the owner of the blue boat. We said that we could guide him to Hong Kong if he pulled our junk boat behind his. The kind fisherman had told our boat captain how to get to Hong Kong.

The blue-boat man accepted our offer. This was an awesome deal for us. We were hoping that this new journey with the tiny blue boat would get us to Hong Kong without any more surprises.

CHAPTER 35

The Light at the End of the Tunnel

Our excitement and hope resurged. We put all our belongings back onto the junk boat and waited for the tide to come up. Once the tide was up, the young men and women pushed our junk boat off the sand to get it floating again. The sailors tied a rope from the junk boat to the tiny, light-blue boat. The sound of the light-blue boat's motor gave us the sense that we would have a safer and faster sea journey this time. At last, we were off this lifeless, hellish island. The sea journey so far had felt like an emotional rollercoaster ride from fear, to excitement, to shock.

Being towed was very slow. Even though the blue boat was smaller than our junk boat it was able to pull it steadily. We kept praying that its motor would not fail. Anxiety and worry enveloped our travelling group on the junk boat. There was a growing feeling of sadness and stress inside us all, as we didn't know what further things might be in store for us. So far though, we were keeping our spirits up and keeping hopeful. This was the best medicine for us.

Being towed was very smooth for the first six or seven hours of our journey. Thus far, we had not experienced bad situations such as running out of fuel, or having the motor fail, or being robbed by sea pirates.

The weather was co-operating very well so far, but it was extremely muggy. The captain of our junk boat was listening to the radio, with the hope of picking up any radio signals being broadcasted from Hong Kong this would confirm for us that we were near Hong Kong territory. Finally, we picked up a radio signal a voice giving the weather report for Hong Kong. We all got very excited. All our faces lit up with huge smiles!

This was the happiest moment of our lives. We now could see the light at the end of the tunnel. The darkness and evil that we had been living under for the past four months was about to end. We had got through ruthless communist mental torture, starvation, and brutal regulations. We all felt that we would be free again once we made it to Hong Kong.

We all went up to the upper deck of our junk boat and looked in every direction for ships passing by that could help us. Finally, we spotted a large Hong Kong coastguard ship coming our way and sounding its siren. Our captain knew that it was the Hong Kong coastguard because it was flying the Hong Kong flag.

He ordered the tiny light-blue boat to release the rope attached to our boat. Now we were sailing on our own. We waved and yelled to the owner of the tiny light-blue boat a very big "thank-you!" for pulling us to Hong Kong. We told him that we were hoping to see him again in the refugee camp there. We all shouted and waved to the Hong Kong coast guard ship for help celebrating amongst ourselves at the same time. With much thanks to God, we had actually made it to freedom this time!

CHAPTER 36

The Unwelcome Greeting

When the coastguard got closer, they asked us to identify our boat and where we had come from. We told them we were refugees from Vietnam. They also asked us if we had any weapons on board or if anyone needed any immediate medical attention. We told them that we didn't have any weapons on board and that no one was seriously ill.

The coastguard lowered an inflatable rubber boat, and they circled around our junk boat to inspect it. Then they came on board to search for any illegal items. They did not find anything illegal. The coastguards could see that our pole was broken and questioned our captain. "How long did it take you to get here?" a coastguard asked. "It took us a whole week and the boat was drifting by itself," our captain said. "It's hard to believe this junk boat could make it here with a broken sail pole," the coastguard commented.

Finally, the coastguard handed us a rope that was attached to their ship, we tied it onto the junk boat, and they started towing us to Hong Kong harbour. "Hee Haa! Yes, we finally made it out of hell forever!" we shouted. This was real. We had reached the end of the very dark tunnel. We all felt safe and joyful. We could not wait to see Hong Kong, the destination of our dreams our dream of freedom had come alive. Hong Kong was our gateway to a new life.

After two hours of being towed by the coastguard ship, we still hadn't reached Hong Kong. "I hope they are not towing us back to China," I said to myself. Finally, we could see the mountains and the high-rise buildings of the island of Hong Kong. It was Hong Kong for real! I could not wait to have some real food to fill my hungry stomach, and sweet soda to soothe my thirst. I had been dreaming of and longing for these basic necessities of life for a very, very long time! I missed real, tasty meat, food, and drink more than my mother at this moment. For four months of living in communist hell, I felt we all deserved these tasty treats!

The towing was painfully slow, as our junk was old and falling apart. The coastguard had to go slowly so it wouldn't break into pieces in the middle of the sea. Eventually, we got into the harbour and docked by a huge warehouse. I saw countless refugee junk boats docked everywhere in the harbour. Many refugees had arrived before us.

There were a lot of Hong Kong immigration officials and police officers waiting for us at the dock. I heard one of them shouting at our junk boat with a handheld megaphone, "All you people on this boat come up to the dock, right now! Women and children on one side, men on the other side. Listen up carefully, you bunch of idiots, as I do not want to repeat it twice," the immigration officer shouted. "I have to be here working on Sunday because of all of you motherfuckers showing up!" Wow, what a way to welcome us to Hong Kong! That was not a very nice greeting to say the least. We sensed that they didn't like us being in Hong Kong at all. They were mean and rude to us throughout the immigration process, but we sucked it up better than being towed back to the ocean, like the Malaysian coastguards.

They separated me from my sister and put me in a small room by myself; I was so scared and nervous, wondering why they had put me here, alone. They started to interrogate me. They asked me for my name, age, place of birth, and who I was with. They also asked if I had been to China before I had arrived there. The immigration official told me that I better tell them the whole truth of my journey or else they would send me back to Vietnam. They tried to scare and threaten me, and I did feel scared, but I was focused. I was determined to tell them that I hadn't been in China. My sister had told me before we got to Hong Kong that no matter what the Hong Kong officials asked me, to make sure to tell them that I didn't know anything and that I had never been to China otherwise, they would send us back to China. Finally, I made it through the interrogation, and they let me reunite with my sister.

CHAPTER 37

Abused by Camp Guards

Unfortunately, our dream of freedom had not come true it had been shattered by Hong Kong government regulations. They sent all the refugees into a government detention camp. We were locked up and treated like prisoners.

There was no freedom in the camp. The camp's guards held batons, guarding us like criminals. We all had to line up every morning and evening for a headcount. If just one person in our building went missing, everyone had to stay there, standing still, until the guards found the missing person. The missing person would be beaten in the guard's office. Every day, people got punished for not obeying the camp's rules.

I was put to work as a volunteer office cleaner, my sister Allison worked as administrative assistant in the office in the detention camp responsible for processing refugee arrivals, and Minh worked as a camp cleaner. I cleaned the office desks, took out the office garbage, and cleaned the guards' changing room. By doing these jobs, all three of us earned some credits and a good reference for our future immigration applications. My office-cleaner job also earned me extra food for my sister and Minh.

One day, when I was alone, cleaning the guards' changing room, one of the guards came in and took his frustration out on me. He started punching me with his fist and kicking me like a sandbag. I tried to run out the door, but he pulled me back and continued his assault on me for no reason. I begged him to stop hitting me and to let me go.

Luckily, someone else came in, prompting him to stop hitting me, and I managed to get out of the changing room. This physical abuse still haunts me today. I can't forget this incident, and I cannot forgive that asshole camp guard. I kept this incident to myself. I did not tell my sister about this experience. It was just my unlucky day, I guess.

One morning, I discovered some bubbles forming around my fingers. This was very unusual. I did not know what it was, so I did not pay much attention to it. A few days went by and the bubbles started getting bigger and turned yellow! I thought that I might have gotten the measles from some kid. This was not cool at all. The bubbles were very itchy and very painful, with pus bursting out of them.

It was so embarrassing to walk around and be seen by people in the camp. I felt and looked like a zombie. Everybody tried to stay away from me. Measles is highly contagious. My sister took me to the camp medical clinic to get some antibiotics.

CHAPTER 38

Summary of Suffering

It took a few weeks for the measles to go away. It was yet more unwanted suffering on this hellish journey. Why was there so much suffering for me, at the age of thirteen?

Month after month of living on the run, living from house to houses belonging to total strangers to meal most starving, almost losing my life twice once from drowning and once from malaria the horrific murder of my only close friend Dory, my sister nearly getting raped by our cousin's friend, nearly dying when our junk boat almost broke apart in a storm in the middle of the sea, and stranded and starving on a deserted island for a few days without any food: these were all horrific, hellish experiences. Then we had miraculously landed in Hong Kong, the so-called land of freedom.

However, this land did not give us freedom. We were placed in a detention camp locked up and treated like criminals in jail. I felt safer in Hong Kong than in China, but still I had been physically abused by one of the camp guards for no good reason.

And as if this wasn't bad enough, now I had to suffer for a few weeks with the measles! The suffering wasn't just physical, also mental and emotional, as all of the other refugees in the camp avoided me I had hives all over my body, and they were afraid to catch measles and become ill like me. As a result of this, I was a loner in the camp with no friends and no companionship. This was harsh for me, and there was nobody to help me through this suffering as my sister and Minh were too busy working in the detention camp.

Many people in the camp felt humiliated by the camp guards and received punishment deserved only by criminals, not by desperate and helpless refugees. The refugees became so tired of mistreatment that they united in defiance of these abuses and set the camp on fire to get the attention of the United Nations. We wanted them to hear of our frustration and suffering in the detention camp.

We were trying to tell the media that we had travelled to Hong Kong to escape inhumane torture from the communist regime in Vietnam and to gain true freedom, but now we had all ended up in jail, in the supposedly "free territory" of Hong Kong. What was the difference between our treatment by the Hong Kong government and the communist regime back in Vietnam?

Refugees threw rocks, glass bottles, and metal sticks at the camp guards attacking them from all directions. The camp guards retreated back to their office and called in the riot police, to rescue them. That was when the media was notified about the riot and came to the camp to film it.

The mental suffering in the detention camp was immeasurable. We were innocent and helpless refugees we did not deserve to be punished like criminals. It was unjust.

CHAPTER 39

Real Freedom Arrives

The riot police came and restored order in the camp. They also captured some of the demonstrators and locked down our camp lodgings. No one was allowed to leave their quarters until the camp officials could figure out why the riot had started. We were under a curfew for the whole day. I was scared and nervous. I was worried that we might get locked up at a tougher, stricter detention camp.

We didn't know if we would ever get out of there, but by the next day everything seemed to have cooled down. The camp guards did not come to do their usual morning headcount. The riot seemed to have scared them, as they were treating us much better. The situation in the camp was calmer now.

A week passed by, then representatives from the United Nations (UN) arrived and started to hand out applications to the refugees, allowing the refugees to choose which country they wanted to settle in.

At that time, Australia, France, Norway, and Canada were accepting refugees from Vietnam. My mother had suggested that we seek refuge in the United States, but due to the political conflict with communists in Vietnam and China, plus the absence of an immigration representative from the USA in Hong Kong, we had to make a choice. We desperately wanted to get out of this nightmare for good.

My sister and Minh were looking for any country that ensured freedom, so we chose Canada. Soon after, we handed in our application for immigration to Canada and we received an acceptance letter from Immigration Canada. We believe that we were accepted so quickly by the Government of Canada because of a good reference from the camp officials, as all three of us performed well in our volunteer work positions in the camp. Now the true, precious gift of freedom had finally arrived. The suffering had ended. This was the greatest joy of our lives!

Although my sister and I had made it out of hell and were rejoicing because of our acceptance into Canada, my mother was experiencing great distress back in Vietnam; my sister and I had been away from Vietnam for eight months, and my mother had no idea whether we were still alive, as we had had no way of communicating with her. She cried every time she thought of us. She was extremely frustrated that the Vietnamese communist regime did not allow any form of communication between Vietnamese citizens and their family members outside of Vietnam. All of the letters that I mailed to my mother, letting her know that Allison and I were safe and had been accepted for immigration to Canada, were never received: they were intercepted and destroyed.

CHAPTER 40

Freedom is Priceless

Anxiously waiting at home for any news of her two absent children was heartbreaking for my mother. I had no doubt she was constantly thinking, wondering, and worrying about our safety. This tore her heart apart, as we had been away from home for about a year now and she hadn't heard a word from us. The suspense was killing her.

The Vietnamese communist regime was crushing the South Vietnamese people, making people's lives progressively more miserable by the day. The South Vietnamese people became extremely poor and had great difficulty obtaining the basic necessities of life. Thus, my mother decided to leave Vietnam even though she didn't know where Allison and I were.

My mother decided to take the sea route to Indonesia, through the South China Sea in the hope of avoiding Thai waters, where Thai sea pirates were robbing, raping, and killing Vietnamese refugees sailing to freedom in neighbouring countries. She travelled with my two younger brothers, my older sister, and my aunt.

Unfortunately, despite avoiding Thai waters, my mother's refugee boat was still intercepted by Thai sea pirates. They robbed of all the refugees on board, leaving them with no valuables. Perhaps contents with their spoils, the pirates did not rape any of the women, or drown any of the men. That was very lucky for my mom's boat. The pirates seemed happy with what they had taken.

Luckily, their boat made it safely to Indonesia and my mother, my two younger brothers, my older sister, and my aunt were put into a refugee camp on an Indonesian island. They would end up spending approximately eight months in this Indonesian refugee camp before being accepted for immigration to the USA.

At last, Allison and I were able to reconnect with our mother. A friend of my mother's, in Paris, France, acted as a liaison between us, helping us to let her know we were alive. My mother now lives in Houston, Texas.

It's quite a miracle that everyone in our family survived hell and is now extremely happy, living in truly free countries. Despite all the sacrifices, the traumatic experiences, and the suffering we had to endure on our horrific journey for freedom, it was absolutely worth it! Freedom is truly priceless! Never do I want to lose it again.

Quoc An (Andy) Lieu.

andylieu2003@yahoo.ca

ABOUT THE AUTHOR

My Children's Horrific Journey to Freedom is Andy Lieu's first book. Born in Vietnam, he now lives with his wife, son, and daughter in Vancouver, British Columbia, where he enjoys the freedom he strove so hard to attain.

Printed in Canada